Domes of America

PHOTOGRAPHS BY ERIC OXENDORF

TEXT BY WILLIAM SEALE

An Archetype Press Book

POMEGRANATE ARTBOOKS • SAN FRANCISCO

PUBLISHED BY
POMEGRANATE ARTBOOKS
Box 6099
Rohnert Park, California
94927-6099

PRODUCED BY
ARCHETYPE PRESS, INC.
WASHINGTON, D.C.
Project Director: Diane Maddex
Art Director: Marc A. Meadows
Assistant Graphic Designers:
Robert L. Wiser, Melton Castro

LIBRARY OF CONGRESS
CATALOGING-IN-
PUBLICATION DATA
Seale, William.
Domes of America / photographs by Eric Oxendorf; text by William Seale.
p.   cm.
ISBN 0-87654-070-1
1. Domes — United States.
2. United States — Capital and capitol.
I. Oxendorf, Eric. II. Title
NA2890.S42 1994   94-7930
725'.11'0973 — dc20   CIP

98 97 96 95 94 5 4 3 2 1

PRINTED IN CHINA

PHOTOGRAPHS
Page 1: Milwaukee County Public Library (1895, Ferry and Clas), Milwaukee, Wisconsin

Page 2: Woodbury County Courthouse (1916–18, William L. Steele), Sioux City, Iowa

Page 6: Brown County Courthouse (1910, Charles E. Bell), Green Bay, Wisconsin

Page 10: Old St. Louis County Courthouse (1839–62, Henry Singleton, William Rumbold, R. S. Mitchell, et al.), St. Louis, Missouri

Page 17: Baltimore City Hall (1867–75, George A. Frederick), Baltimore, Maryland

Page 108: San Francisco City Hall (1913–15, John Bakewell, Jr., and Arthur Brown, Jr.), San Francisco, California

Contents

HONORABLE INDUSTRY ALWAYS TRAVELS
THE SAME ROAD WITH ENJOYMENT AND DUTY.

COMMERCE AND AGRICULTURE FLOURISH
WHEREVER AND WHENEVER THERE IS PEACE.

THERE IS NO VIRTUE SO TRULY GREAT
AND GOD LIKE, AS JUSTICE.

Preface

ERIC OXENDORF

While I was lying on the cool marble under the dome of the Rhode Island State Capitol, a state patrol officer and another man walked up to me. "What are you doing?" the man inquired. I gave some glib response, they laughed, and then they walked away. A few minutes later the officer returned. "It was nice of you," he said, "to start the governor's day with a smile."

What I was doing was photographing the dome. As a photographer specializing in architectural and industrial subjects, I often travel throughout the country and give myself little photography assignments to keep myself visually alert—such as European doorknobs, color combinations, and construction-site humor. Photographing state capitol domes is one of those self-appointed tasks that found its way to a poster and now a book.

The idea of photographing domes came to me as I was driving to a week-long project in Florida in 1985. On a boring stretch of I-65 in Indiana, I started quizzing myself about the locations of the state capitals. When I reached Indianapolis, I stopped to take a look at the statehouse. Walking into the rotunda, I knew that I had found a new assignment. The power and the history of these public spaces became clear to me.

That first dome photograph in Indiana set the scope for this series: I would use the same camera and lens, set the tripod the same distance from the floor, and take each view "as is," without added lighting. Later, down the road on the way to the Kentucky State Capitol, I decided to photograph only capitol buildings.

The Kentucky rotunda gave me the first major problem: a statue of Lincoln in the middle of the floor. Next came Tennessee, Georgia, and Alabama, followed by Florida. There it was a question of whether to shoot the old or the new capitol. I opted for the old, as I did later in Louisiana. Like Kentucky, the capitols in Connecticut, California, Illinois, Virginia, North Carolina, and Georgia also had statues or other monuments in their rotundas, making it impossible to get a centered view of the dome.

Not all the state capitols are here, for the simple reason that not all of them have domes. Other places were included because they met the specifications for a majestic interior space—with a dome—and because I wanted to expand the scope of the project. For the first few years I would photograph a dome if I was within a hundred miles of it. However, when my patient editor, Diane Maddex, reminded me of deadlines, I ended up flying to seven sites to complete this collection.

As time went on people became interested and even excited about what I was doing. It amazed me that many of them had never pondered what was overhead until they saw someone on the floor looking up. At the U.S. Capitol there were hordes of people. After I filled out forms, got checked out by the security department, and then was escorted to the rotunda, two officers shielded me from the curious mob until my images were made. As soon as I had packed up and walked away, a dozen people fell on the floor to get the same view with their snapshot cameras.

The last dome I photographed was the Milwaukee County Public Library in my hometown. I had passed under this rotunda for years. When I was seven years old I would sneak in and spend entire days there during the summer. We lived only eight blocks away, but I could visit the world through its books.

These domes carry some interesting secrets. Sound reverberations are unexpected—a whisper is no longer a whisper. I found this out as I mumbled to myself while solving various technical problems. In Hawaii the capitol has an open rotunda; its dome is the sky you see in the photograph. Some domes had birds, and some had bats—there's a story for every location.

Nothing especially creative was required to make these images. I was a technician who analyzed the lighting, set up the equipment, dealt with logistical problems, and transferred an image of a beautiful three-dimensional space onto a two-dimensional piece of film. All the photographs were made with a Hasselblad swc/m with an f4.5 Zeiss Biogon lens and an aperture of f/8. The legs of the tripod, a Gitzo Studex with an r2 head, were at the normal collapsed position; the camera was mounted thirty inches from the floor. Regardless of the light source, the following Kodak 120 films were used: Kodak Plus-x Pan (iso 100) black-and-white (hc-110 dil. b process); Kodak Vericolor iii-s daylight color negative (c-41 process); Kodak Vericolor ii-l color negative (c-41 process); Kodak Ektachrome (ept-160) color transparency; Kodak Ektachrome, mostly Ektachrome Plus (epp-100) or Lumiere (lpp-100), depending on availability and latest technology (e-6 process); and Polaroid Polacolor 669 or Polapan 100 with Hasselblad Polaroid 100 film back. Locations shot first were photographed without filters, but as more pl-22 fluorescent or mercury vapor lighting was found, a cc20m (magenta) or cc30m filter generally was used. Lighting was natural, as found. Minimal adjustments were made to each site, except that burned-out light bulbs were replaced when possible.

As in any project of this scope and this many miles, there are many people to thank, especially the capitol architects, building engineers, secretaries of state, and security staffs. My thanks are due also for special favors, such as the Nebraska guard who turned on the inaugural chandelier—which is normally lighted only once every four years.

Nearly every dome I photographed led me to another. Their variations were like an architectural kaleidoscope. For a while they became a blur. But now, looking at the entire collection, they produce a feeling of grandeur—a reflection of a time past in our great architectural heritage and a tribute to the artisans who helped make America look the way it does today.

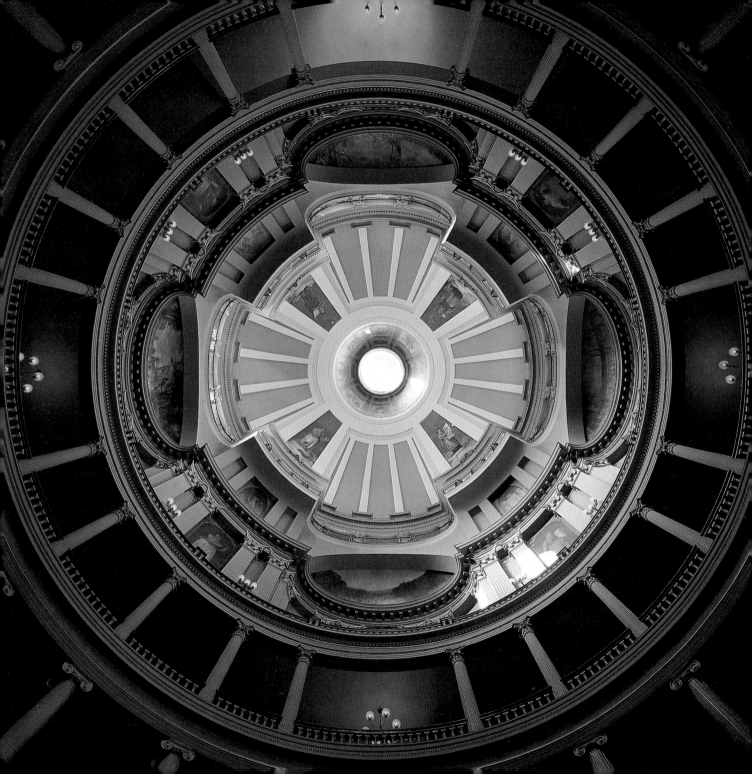

Introduction

WILLIAM SEALE

To Americans the dome is the architectural symbol of democracy. Rising over the prairies or from the hearts of cities, it announces the presence of a government as clearly as a steeple proclaims a church. This book presents a selection of American domes. Most of them crown state capitols, where they have been built consciously as symbols of government. Here you see them inside and from below—the camera's eye looking up into their shells, where the hemispherical shape and the play of light make the dome work a special magic that has fascinated humankind for several thousand years.

A dome by definition is a circular vault. A vault is a masonry arch or a combination of arches that spans a space to cover it without columns or other central vertical supports; the arches throw the weight to side piers or walls. The earliest known example of the art of vaulting is from the seventh century B.C., a simple arched structure of bricks protecting a drainage ditch at Nimrod in Mesopotamia. Obviously it was not the first. The later Greeks knew the principles of round-arch vaulting, but stepped or corbeled vaults were used long before. Over centuries, need and taste have inspired probably more than a hundred variations on the vault. The dome is the most ambitious.

A dome can be as simple as an igloo or a bake oven of mud or bricks, or as grand as the architectural crown of a church or a capitol. Strictly speaking, it is built of solid masonry and is self-supporting: each part contributes to the stability of the whole. The domes in this book were built with no purpose other than to be beautiful. Builders found ways early on to simplify the requirements for their construction while achieving the same dramatic effect. For centuries the technology advanced slowly, until the nineteenth century.

Iron, steel, reinforced concrete, and hollow-tile structural technology over the past 150 years have made it possible to achieve the dome form without load-bearing construction.

Before imperial Rome, vaulting had been hidden away. Romans brought structural detailing out in the open as a feature of design, and it was they who gave the dome its first glory. Their public buildings were characterized by vaults of brick, stone, and concrete mortared, like their walls, with *pozzolana*, the powerful Roman cement made of volcanic ash and lime. Roman builders took delight in buildings that expressed strength and endurance. They favored barrel vaults—continuous, tunnel-like arching—for both corridors and rooms and formed fireproof groin vaults where two barrel vaults crossed and spanned square and rectangular spaces. As Roman civil engineering advanced, builders frequently modified the groin vault by substituting a simpler system of intersecting arches or ribs that carried the load and infill elsewhere in place of solid masonry; the groined appearance was preserved, but the cost was less. The vault was filled in above and behind with rubble.

The dome was the next step in structural challenge. It was entirely round. In theory it consisted of a trim, self-supporting system of wedge-shaped stones resting on one another—in no need of mortar—rising to an apex. The circular, vertical walls that held it up from beneath, called the drum, contained through-arching and other concealed strengthening devices to contradict the dome's natural outward force against it. The apparent structural virtuoso of the dome is as much a part of its appeal as the actual form.

Dome technology advanced to rib construction, consisting of a union of arches springing from a round base and creating the bones of a bowl or saucer shape, the areas in between filled with lighter materials. Before the reign of Emperor Hadrian (117–38 A.D.), Roman domes were mostly half domes in niches. Full domes were first known in garden houses during the empire, for their beauty, and in steam baths or *calidaria*, for their practicality. In the

Pantheon in Rome, completed by Hadrian in 125 A.D. and possibly even designed by him, the dome made its debut as a principal feature in public architecture. One hundred forty-four feet in diameter, the great dome is a circular vault built of brick and concrete, with a vast central oculus open to the sky. The only survivor intact of the great public buildings of imperial Rome, the Pantheon is one of the significant achievements in the architecture of the world.

Three hundred years later the Byzantine Empire created its greatest architectural monument, the Church of St. Sophia in Constantinople. Here the dome rises with bravado over a square room. Pendentives curve upward bracketlike from the corners, meeting the hundred-foot diameter of the lower ring of the dome; the eye travels up into the dome's interior, which is splendidly decorated in gold and colors and crossed by light. Through the following thousand years in Egypt and Turkey, Persia and India, the dome continued as a feature of religious architecture. It was probably the Muslims who introduced the onion-shaped variation.

In the Renaissance in Europe, notably in Italy, the dome proclaimed the glory of God in the landscape for miles around. So tall was it that additional structural ribs and sometimes buttresses were introduced for strength, all becoming part of the external design; so strong was the outward thrust of the dome that the drum had to be strengthened with wooden structural elements, or "chains," to keep the dome from pushing it apart. Renaissance domes appeared variously as wood and as masonry with wooden exteriors. Inner domes lowered the height of the domes and brought them to a scale humans could comprehend without perceiving that they really saw an artificial ceiling.

Three domes built within a span of two centuries from the Renaissance to Louis XIV became the most prominent models for American domes, especially in the nineteenth century. The earliest was designed by Michelangelo for St. Peter's in Rome and completed in 1509 after his death; the other two are later, neoclassical domes: the church of Les Invalides (1706) in Paris, designed by J. H. Mansart; and St. Paul's Cathedral (1710) in London, by Sir Christopher Wren. All church domes, they were taken from their ecclesiastical context to become, in America, governmental symbols.

The dome first appeared on an American capitol in the whimsical wooden dome added to the Maryland Statehouse between 1785 and 1787. In the next decade, after it was settled that a dome would be put on the national capitol-yet-to-be, the commonwealth of Massachusetts built a dome atop its state-house in Boston in 1798 and was followed by Pennsylvania in 1810-21, then North Carolina in 1818–21, both, like Maryland's, with fully developed rotundas. The first dome of the U.S. Capitol in Washington was a latecomer, completed in its early form in 1827 as the bulbous, rather curious design of Charles Bulfinch, who had built the equally bulbous dome on the statehouse in Boston nearly thirty years before. When President Lincoln was inaugurated, work on a new, grander dome of cast iron had stopped because of the approaching war. He ordered it to resume: if people saw the dome going on, he said, they would know that the Union would continue as well. And as the great dome rose to completion in 1863, in the Civil War's darkest hours, Americans took it to their hearts.

The dome was not an original feature of American state capitol architecture but usurped the place of the colonial cupola and tower. In the two decades before the Civil War the finest state capitol architecture turned from domes back to towers. But the state capitols that followed the war, up to World War 1, had monumental domes, cribbed in fact from Washington, St. Peter's, or Les Invalides. The dome was challenged with the Nebraska capitol, designed in 1919 and completed in 1932, which turned the sensibilities of capitol builders to towers once again. In West Virginia is to be found the single exception: a perfect neo-Renaissance pile topped by an adaptation of the dome of St. Paul's. The state of Oklahoma, half finished building its capitol at the time the dome fell from favor around World War I, cancelled plans for a dome—and the capitol in Oklahoma City remains hatless today.

Most American laws are made beneath domes, as are laws in many other countries, imitating the American idea. These domes come in many costumes. Some are simple inside, their shells painted plaster, while others are elaborate. In the following pages are domes resplendent with decorative glass that is clear, etched, cut, or stained; triumphant with allegorical murals showing nymphs and cherubs bearing constitutions and law books; splendid with sculpture in plaster or marble and richly cast and carved ornamentation covered with gold leaf. The sun shines down through the central open "eye," or oculus, at the highest point, or from the windows of a lantern or cupola of glass surmounting the dome. Watch for the different means the designers have used to control light and turn it to their purposes within the dome. For all the efforts made to incorporate artificial light, it is still natural light that, when managed, serves a dome best.

Eric Oxendorf's domes are a unique architectural photography project. Traveler and artist, Oxendorf has focused on the one image that most strongly represents the dome: his camera is aimed up from the floor into the domes' inner shells. The height needed for external effect is never necessary inside, so it is a lowered false ceiling one sees from the rotunda. Straight-on views such as Oxendorf has taken normally come only in passing glimpses upward. Busy, crowded rotundas and watchful guards discourage people from lying on their backs on the rotunda floor, although a bold Oxendorf did this. Domes are more typically remembered seen on the move and at angles.

Removed from their visual context, Oxendorf's domes become two-dimensional designs purely in themselves—rather like quilts on a clothesline or artists' studies encased in folios. His subject, collectively, is a chorus of civic pride expressed by generations of Americans through one of architecture's most beautiful forms.

U.S. Capitol

This grandest of American domes was designed in 1855 and completed in 1863, the work of Thomas U. Walter, architect of the capitol's expansion. Just a few years after the constitution was adopted, the founders of the new nation conceived the idea of a rotunda with a dome, a central space envisioned for public sessions of the governing bodies — much as Hadrian had used the Pantheon. A quarter century after its completion in 1829, the crowded capitol was too small to serve its functions. Under Walter, who held the position of architect of the capitol, and army engineer Capt. Montgomery C. Meigs the building gained vast wings to the north and south. To unify the architectural composition, Walter devised a grand dome based on the contemporary iron dome of St. Isaac's in Moscow, ribbed with iron and covered by iron plates cast in architectural forms, all painted white. Constantino Brumidi, the "Michelangelo of the Capitol," adorned the dome's oculus and surrounding walls with allegorical paintings: At the center, 180 feet up, is The Apotheosis of George Washington, completed in 1865; Liberty and Victory flank the president and are joined in the fresco by fourteen female figures representing the original states and the Union. Beyond them are images of the arts and sciences, the sea, commerce, mechanics, and agriculture. Beginning in 1877 Brumidi continued his work beyond the coffered ceiling, on a lower ring three hundred feet around that portray four hundred years of history. The exterior of this great dome first became the symbol of union during the Civil War, its outline towering against the American sky.

WASHINGTON, D.C. 1793–1865

19

Library of Congress

The Main Reading Room, whose octagonal shape was determined by Librarian of Congress A. R. Spofford, is graced with this splendid domed ceiling. Spofford, librarian from 1878 to 1897, was a leading light in the planning and design of the library's new building, which replaced the former library located in the U.S. Capitol. Spofford retired in 1897, the year in which the building was occupied. Architects John L. Smithmeyer and Paul Pelz borrowed heavily from the Paris Opera House for the exterior and in the classification of spaces within. The Reading Room, for all its grandeur, seems quiet and secluded after being approached through magnificent marble stairhalls. Like the building's other public spaces, the room is rich in artwork. The eight classifications of books in the library, developed by Spofford, are identified by allegorical sculptures high on the dome's drum, the work of various sculptors, including Louis Saint-Gaudens, Daniel Chester French, and Paul W. Bartlett. Edwin H. Blashfield painted the Evolution of Civilization around the collar of the dome, depicted as twelve figures representing twelve historic epochs. Floating above all, in the dome's lantern, is Human Understanding, a female figure who lifts her veil while attended by cherubs. Albert Weinert's deep plaster coffers in the ceiling, inset with rosettes, diminish in size toward the top of the golden dome. There is no more splendid interior space in Washington than this—not even the rotunda of the capitol.

WASHINGTON, D.C. 1886–97

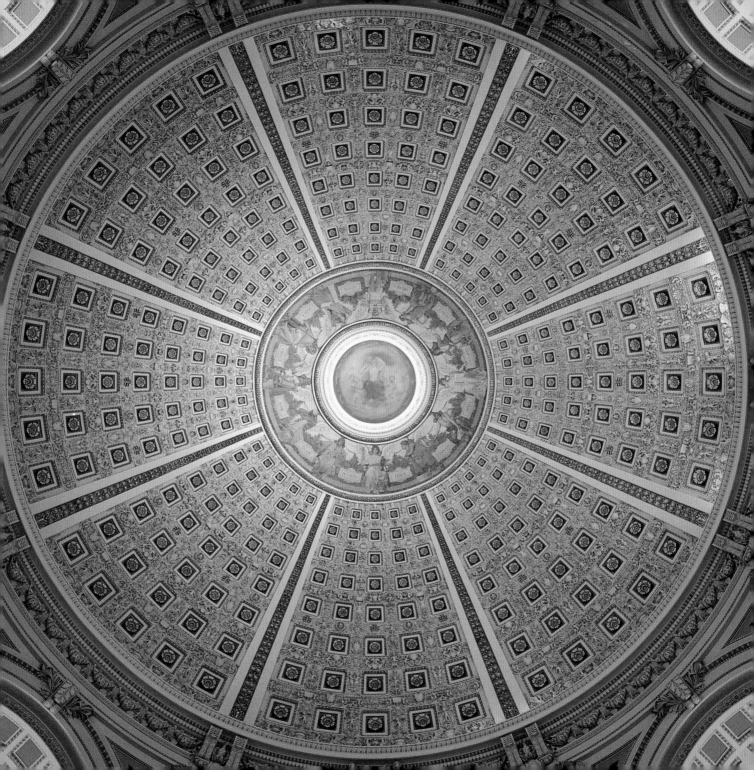

Alabama State Capitol

Although this dome was built in the early 1850s, it did not receive its decorative painting until just before World War I. The interior originally may have been white or white with gold highlighting. Erected after its predecessor burned, the building survives almost uniquely as a vernacular statehouse having more connection to old county courthouse forms than to most state capitols. Here on February 18, 1861, Jefferson Davis was inaugurated as president of the Confederacy, and in this building the rebel government operated in its early months, before moving on to Richmond. The Alabama capitol was expanded to the sides at the turn of the century but remained in a remarkable state of preservation in 1987, when a full-scale restoration and further expansion began. Historical echoes are powerful in this building, particularly in its legislative halls, now restored to the time when the Confederacy was born. Murals in the dome's shell by Roderick McKenzie, painted in 1930, tell Alabama's story. On the capitol's lawns and on Decatur Avenue in front, the civil rights movement burst into full bloom under Martin Luther King, Jr., in the 1960s. King's church still stands across the street. From this ring of rotunda balconies spectators watched the development of both epochs in American history.

MONTGOMERY. 1851

23

Arizona State Capitol

Built at the turn of the century and designed by Texas architect Gordon J. Riley, the Arizona capitol is still in use for government purposes, although legislative deliberations were moved to annex buildings in the late 1950s. This building spent much of its life disliked. Among those who would have preferred to replace it was Frank Lloyd Wright, who, from his desert enclave near Scottsdale, planned a dreamlike capitol he called Oasis, hoping to attract legislators who were seriously debating how to expand the existing capitol. Riley's capitol, a popular building now restored, seems almost miniature compared to capitols in neighboring states. Yet it is in every sense a capitol, with as many monumental effects as the architect could persuade his clients to build. The rotunda rises into a dome that is clearly defined on the outside—but more lantern than dome inside—carrying the eye up, through geometric forms that frame a central chandelier, into an oculus of stained glass.

PHOENIX. 1899–1900

Arkansas State Capitol

Built by the time of World War I, the Arkansas capitol was a ship on a stormy political sea for most of the years it was under way. Construction stopped and resumed. The architect, George R. Mann, was replaced by the more famous architect Cass Gilbert; but the man in charge was Gov. George W. Donaghey, who made a number of mistakes, notable among which was his failure to site the structure on direct axis with the street it faces, leaving the great pile crooked to the grid of Little Rock. It is a capitol of grand Beaux Arts ambitions, its interior built of marble from Vermont, Colorado, and Alabama. The dome rides on four great arches with pendentives springing from the four corners that appear to support the dome over the square space in the manner of St. Sophia's. The dome itself follows St. Paul's: the drum ringed by a colonnade, with a lantern atop. Steel framing was used extensively here. From the oculus of the dome hangs a brass chandelier said to weigh two tons; created for the building by L. C. Tiffany Studios, it has smaller mates in the house and senate. Governor Donaghey commemorated his role in building the capitol by cutting a walnut tree his father had planted as a youth and having it made into a conference table that is still in the governor's office.

LITTLE ROCK. 1899–1917

California State Capitol

When the project to build a capitol was begun in the mid-1850s, California was not even a decade removed from the Gold Rush. A design completed in 1856 proposed a building like the Mississippi capitol, built two decades before; indeed, Ruben Clark, who drew the plan, had served as a carpenter on that construction. With the outbreak of the Civil War, officials threw out Clark's plan and had him redraw it, with subsequent improvements by G. P. Cummings, to suggest the remodeled national capitol in Washington with its great dome. This was the first instance in which a state consciously imitated the U.S. Capitol. There would be many to come. As the California capitol neared its century mark, dangers from earthquakes threatened it and led to a major restoration and seismic retrofitting. The dome is seen here in its restored splendor, rising above a marble allegory of California.

SACRAMENTO. 1864

Colorado State Capitol

Among the architects of post–Civil War America who spangled the American landscape with state capitols was Elijah E. Myers, who started work as a carpenter in Philadelphia and established himself in the Midwest as an architect in the late 1860s. Colorado's is the last of Myers's capitols, although during its long years of construction Myers left the project and died in its last year. His design was followed fairly closely. It was a building out of style when completed, standing in a city that, although resplendent with Victorian architecture, by 1909 favored visionary city planning and the neoclassicism espoused at the World's Columbian Exposition of 1893. The dome is a typical Myers spectacle, seen similarly in Michigan and Texas. Constructed of painted cast iron, it rises through stages to dizzying height and is crossed by daylight from rings of windows. When it was completed the dome was covered with copper, and the public rose in protest that copper meant Montana, not Colorado. To calm the storm the governor ordered the dome covered with Colorado gold. Within the rotunda, which rises 180 feet, are murals by Allen True from 1940 and poetic inscriptions by Thomas H. Ferril. "Beyond the Sundown," writes Ferril, "is tomorrow's Wisdom. Today is going to be long ago."

DENVER. 1886–1909

Connecticut State Capitol

Built from the designs of noted architect Richard M. Upjohn, the Connecticut capitol was an architectural event in its time—started in the year of a national panic. It is Gothic Revival in style, built of stone, with fortresslike construction. Originally it was to have had no dome, only a tower appropriate to a Gothic building. This did not rest well with the capitol commissioners, most of them veterans of the Union Army; the chief engineer, a powerful figure, was Gen. William B. Franklin, who had worked on the U.S. Capitol. These patriots demanded and at last won their dome, which the architect added during construction; he supported it on heavy piers that intrude visibly on the central space shown here. The dome is fully detailed in the Gothic manner and elongated as much as Upjohn dared to also suggest a tower. Looking up into its interior, above the cast of the statue Genius of Connecticut, commissioned for the building by the state government in 1876, the spatial episodes suggest the interior of a lantern more than a dome. The Connecticut capitol, endangered for many years, was recently restored to the blazing glory of the Gilded Age— named by its neighbor up the street, Mark Twain.

HARTFORD. 1873–79

Old Florida State Capitol

Florida's old capitol originally looked like the large house of a successful planter—essentially a rectangle enhanced by four-columned porticoes front and back. Built from designs by Cary Butt of Mobile, it stood for more than a half century before being expanded in 1901 and again in the 1920s, when it gained a more traditional, domed appearance. In the late 1960s its future was debated at an odd time in the history of state capitol buildings: historic preservation had not yet made its case, and architects and contractors saw business opportunities in sagging statehouses. No capitols had been built anywhere for forty years. Then the new capitol in Honolulu and ones proposed for Juneau and Phoenix excited the spirit of monument building. Florida's capitol was scheduled for demolition, and in 1978 a skyscraper statehouse with embracing wings was completed behind the original building. Time intervened, and public opposition to tearing down the old capitol became so strong that restoration was undertaken by architect Hershel Shephard in 1982. Returned to its appearance early in the century, the capitol now is complete with linoleum floors and ceiling fans, as well as plaster walls and ceilings painted in the Pompeiian colors used in 1901. Its simple paneled dome of plaster lights a large, square stairhall on the second floor—lanternlike, its oculus shining with turn-of-the-century stained glass.

TALLAHASSEE. 1841–45, 1901, 1921

Georgia State Capitol

When this statehouse was completed in 1889, Atlanta had only recently been designated the capital. The city was central to the New South movement and modeled itself on Chicago. A Chicago architectural firm, Edbrooke and Burnham, was employed to give the city a fine midwestern-type capitol. The dome is loosely based on Les Invalides and rests atop a tall drum that is lengthened visually inside by a ring of paired pilasters and tall openings. With a lantern topping the dome, light is admitted at the sides instead of through an oculus. Inside the rotunda the dome seems distant from the floor, very narrow, and rather apart from the interior. The capitol itself is downtown, on a small parcel of land, and rises barely seen in the midst of modern skyscrapers that have—as in most capital cities—overwhelmed the once-dominant dome.

ATLANTA. 1884–89

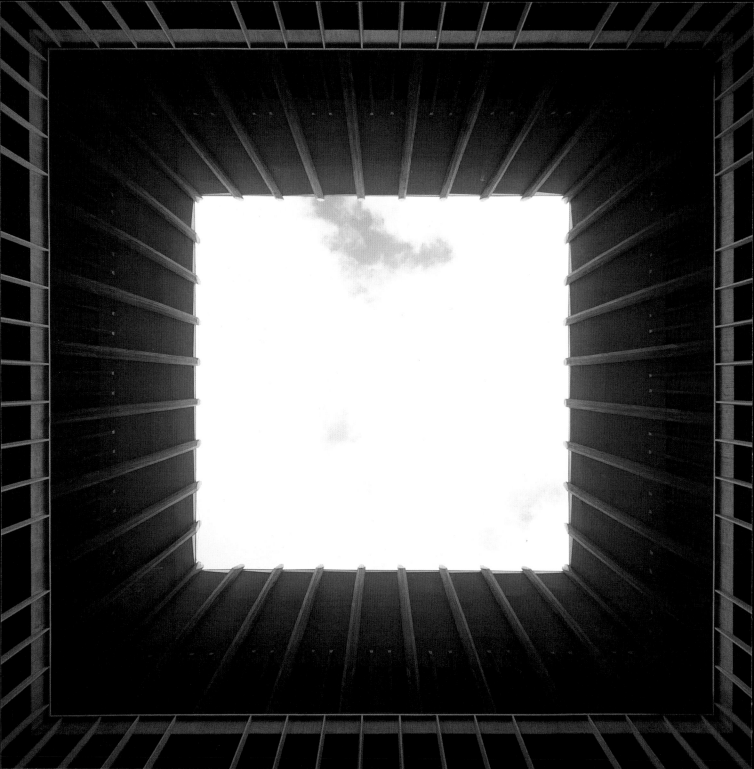

Hawaii State Capitol

America's newest capitol was completed a decade after statehood to be occupied by the legislature of the new state of Hawaii. Belt, Lemmon and Lo and John Carl Warnecke intended the building for a point in Honolulu Harbor, surrounded on three sides by water and visible to people arriving by air, the usual approach to Hawaii today. Public sentiment for the historic grounds of Iolani Palace, sacred to native Hawaiians and a symbol for all Hawaii, eventually won out; the capitol stands not far from the old palace of the Hawaiian kings, which was built in 1883 and is nestled into the city more than the designers wished. The central area, where in most capitols the rotunda would be, is large and open in the sense that the Pantheon is open. A dense pattern of ribs on an upward curving roof suggests traditional structural character. While the building strikingly recalls the islands' palm-roofed houses, it was meant to suggest the geological birth of Hawaii—volcanoes rising from the sea. The capitol is set in a pool, the open space seen here placed between two mountainlike structures of stone that contain the legislative chambers. The opening to the sky rises through the uppermost level, which houses the governor's office. Not thirty years of age, the Hawaiian capitol has held its own. Although it misses its harbor site, to be sure, the aging of its materials, the simplicity of its symbolism, and the delight of walking its windswept public areas combine to make it one of the most memorable of all state capitols.

HONOLULU. 1969

Idaho State Capitol

Begun in 1912, the Idaho capitol was built in stages, the last part completed in 1920 and at the time called Renaissance in style. The building is dominated by its dome outside and in, where the vast space rises in successive balcony rings, resplendent with scagliola colonnades, pilasters, and balustrades, dazzling in its whiteness. The clear, bright daylight for which the area is known pours in through windows and skylights and shines in the shellacked surfaces. At night light bulbs, outlining the rings, provide a show. Boise architect J. E. Tourtellotte, who designed the building, made much of the whiteness of the rotunda: "Are the ideals of the people of Idaho morally white and pure?" If so, then "the great white light of conscience must be allowed to shine and by its interior illumination make clear the path of duty. . . . " When the dome glows at night, especially through the snow, it recalls the architect's particular reach for civic symbolism.

BOISE. 1912–20

Illinois State Capitol

This grand statehouse, begun in 1869, replaced the old Greek Revival capitol up the street where Lincoln had served in the legislature. Its origin was unusual. The building stands on land purchased hastily by Springfield developers for a tomb for Lincoln; rejected by the widow in preference for a cemetery, the developers soon transferred the property to the state for a capitol site. This was the first of the great midwestern capitols that were to be built from the 1870s through the 1890s, and its influence can be seen in all of them as well as farther west, in Texas and Colorado. J. C. Cochrane designed the building, with apparently more than a little assistance from two employees, Alfred H. Piquenard, a civil engineer trained at the Ecole Centrale in France, and George C. Garnsey, who later claimed that he had executed the entire design. The Illinois capitol established on paper—for it was not completed for twenty years—a glittery prototype in capitol building that is the most vivid architectural definition of the Gilded Age. Spangled with elaborate architectural detailing rendered in endless variation, the dome in Springfield takes advantage of modern technology, incorporating every short cut and device available to simplify production and reduce costs, while still projecting a traditional image. Built of brick, veneered with stone and pressed tin, warmed by huge steam systems, ventilated, plumbed, and lighted by gas, this state capitol has a thundering majesty expressed perfectly in its soaring rotunda.

SPRINGFIELD. 1869–89

Indiana State Capitol

Times for architects were tough in 1877, when a design competition was held for the Indiana capitol. From a storm of lawsuits and accusations, the building commission emerged with a plan by Adolf Scherrer, a Swiss who was a draftsman in the office of a local architect, Edwin May. The designer had practiced in Europe, and the influence of work over the past decade in Vienna is particularly clear in this capitol, notably in the academic character of the neoclassical motifs and the bold, close massing of the blocks that make up the architectural body of the structure. Set on a constricted site downtown—only one monumental feature of many in Indianapolis's playful city plan of circles—the capitol became part of the cityscape, not its master, as was the case elsewhere. Neither is the rotunda the main feature of the interior; this lofty but relatively simple space shares the glory with vaulted hallways, rich statuary, and carefully designed architectural decoration of the Renaissance style that characterizes the Ringstrasse in Vienna.

INDIANAPOLIS. 1877–88

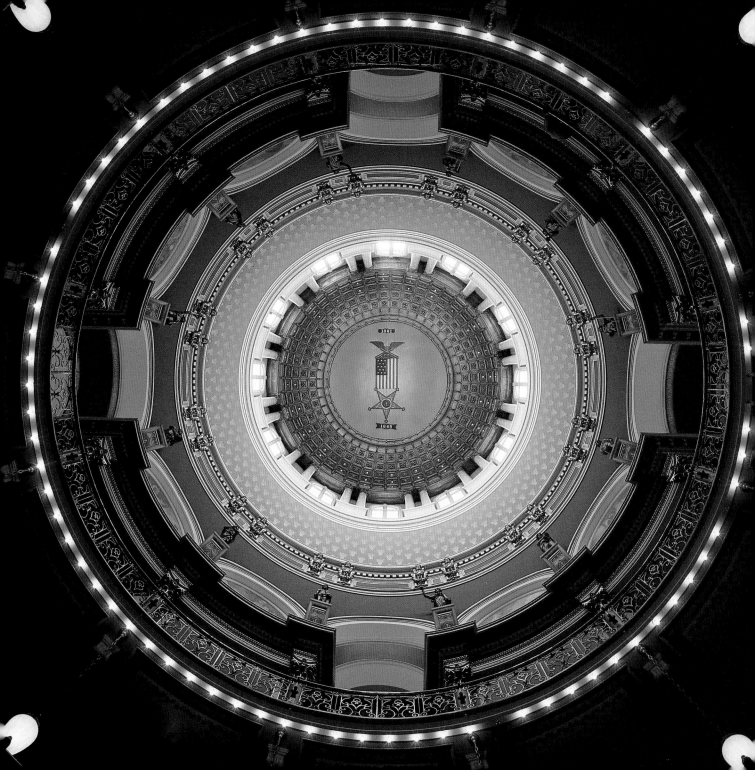

Iowa State Capitol

Designed in 1872 by J. C. Cochrane and Alfred H. Piquenard, who were building the Illinois capitol, Iowa's statehouse plays to the rolling, open landscape
with five domes: one in the center and four smaller domes on corner towers.
Piquenard took the leading role in this capitol, for Cochrane—really more a
businessman than an architect anyway—returned to Chicago after the great
fire of 1871 to make a fortune from the rebuilding. All the elements of the midwestern capitol type are present here. The inner shell of the dome is elaborated
with statuary and decorative painting. Iron, tin, and plaster suggest carved
stone, while paint and metallic powders further disguise them. It is the four
domelets of the corners that set this capitol apart from the others. All five
domes are trimmed in gold leaf and seem to dance whimsically above Des
Moines—an ornament to the city as well as the symbol of state government.

DES MOINES. 1872–80

Kansas State Capitol

Topeka was a raw town when the state of Kansas set out in 1866 to build its capitol for the ages. The building commissioners, first presented with a Second Empire–style design with a mansard roof, threw it aside and ordered Col. J. G. Haskell, the state architect, to design a building as much as practicable like the capitol in Washington. Kansas was thus the second state, after California, to respond architecturally to the great symbol of the Union. Kansas's program was to build in parts. By 1879 the east wing was completed; the west wing and central block followed over the next three decades. It is one of the best of the state capitols: a combination of simplicity, reflecting the earlier Greek Revival (of which it is somewhat a part); the later Renaissance Revival; and turn-of-the-century academic styles, particularly the treatment of the dome, built after Colonel Haskell and his generation were gone. While the capitol's finest feature may be its Corinthian porticoes of carved limestone, the dome represents the building well. It is the newest feature, completed in 1903, but it retains the character of the combined styles used over the long course of construction. In its scale the rotunda is not overwhelming; in fact, compared to most capitols of its era, it appears modest. On its walls, out of view here, are fine historic paintings, notably John Stuart Curry's famous representation of John Brown.

TOPEKA. 1866–73, 1879, 1891–1903

Kentucky State Capitol

Frankfort is one of the few capitals left in America that retains the small-town quality once characteristic of state capitals. The statehouse, completed in 1910, surveys the valley; from the rim one is on a level with the dome's lantern. It is a memorable sight, and with the exception of one intrusive state office building, the view has been maintained throughout this century. Frank Mills Andrews, who had offices in Dayton, Ohio, and New York, was the architect, designing in the French vein, with a dome modeled on Les Invalides. The highest moments of this building are inside, where the dome is central to a great barrel-vaulted cross-axis and opens up to it. Structural steel and hollow tiles achieve the effect of mighty, load-bearing construction in a truly dramatic combination of lofty vaults, all faced in gray and white marble. Abraham Lincoln, seen in the photograph here, and Henry Clay share the rotunda; along the walls of adjacent, balustraded, open hallways are lesser political luminaries of the state's history.

FRANKFORT. 1905–10

Old Louisiana State Capitol

Mark Twain, who saw this building as a burned shell after the Civil War, wrote of it in contempt, saying that such Gothic piles were all the fault of Sir Walter Scott, who inspired them with his romances. The architect was James Dakin, who completed the Gothic castle in 1849. Invading Union forces burned it to its brick walls in 1862. The building was rebuilt by 1882, but whether the resurrection was in fact a reconstruction or a revision of the original is not known. The old capitol contains a large quantity of exposed cast iron, including the skeleton of its grand surprise: the umbrella dome of colored glass. Sheltering a central saloon with a circular staircase, the dome's design—a kaleidoscopic image frozen—is carried out in sumptuous colors of translucent cathedral glass. The fall of light creates a continuing pageant of red, yellow, blue, and green over the cast-iron railings, stairs, and gaslights below. This capitol witnessed the rise of Huey Long, who by 1930, at the peak of his power, commissioned a new statehouse, built nearby over a period of only nine months. The old capitol became a museum.

BATON ROUGE. 1847–49, 1882

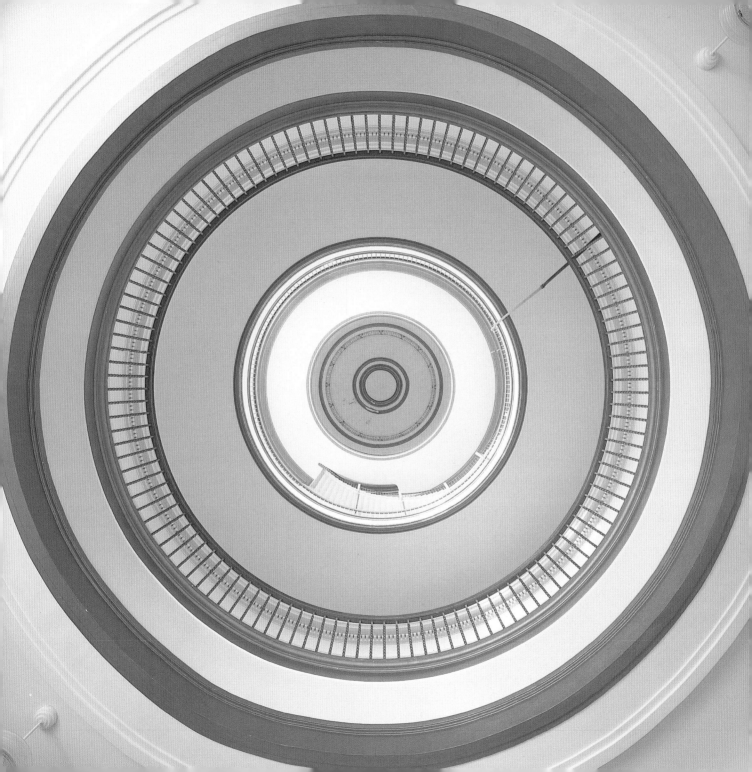

Maine Statehouse

Charles Bulfinch's plans and elevations for Maine's statehouse survive, drawn at the conclusion of his work on the U.S. Capitol and complete with a "temple" or privy at the rear. A major remodeling and an expansion were undertaken by John C. Spofford and Charles Brigham in 1880 and 1891. In 1909–10 the building was demolished except for the portico and rebuilt larger, with steel, by architect G. Henri Desmond. A monumental dome replaced Bulfinch's columned cupola. The statehouse was and is of Hallowell granite, powerfully constructed. The inner shell of the dome is finished in painted plaster and ringed with balconies. The original capitol had no rotunda or saloon, only a central hallway below and the lower house of the legislature above, a plan Bulfinch had introduced in the Boston statehouse. The current Octagonal Hall from 1909–10 gives the sense of a rotunda and is one of the ways Desmond made the building conform to a more typically American capitol form. The simplicity of the building was preserved in the redesign, emphasizing both the fine granite construction and the striking site overlooking the Kennebec River.

AUGUSTA. 1828–31, 1880, 1891, 1909–10

Maryland Statehouse

Whether Maryland's statehouse has a dome or a tower has been a subject of occasional debate for two centuries. Whatever it is called, it is a remarkable confection entirely of wood, completed in 1787 during the confederation period of the American government. This earliest American dome was added to a fine brick statehouse completed three years after the Americans signed their Declaration of Independence. The dome was an improvement the Marylanders hoped would attract Congress to a permanent seat in Annapolis. To at least some of those who built it, the new feature was unquestionably a dome. Joshua Botts, a carpenter, wrote in 1785 that he was going to work for the statehouse builder, Joseph Clark, and put up a "Doom" at wages of "one Dollar a day each of us & Gits our Money Every Saturday Night." The rotunda within is elaborately decorated with cast plaster ornament imitating masonry arches and spandrel vaults; the light plays into an interesting succession of spaces that rise to a domed plaster ceiling. Two centuries later the Maryland statehouse seems almost domestic in scale. The dome seems to float over the city like a ship, set free from its moorings. Even more than the building beneath it, the dome is one of the high points in American architecture of the eighteenth century. It is honored as a bold—indeed a breathless—reach for splendor in the years between the Revolution and the constitution.

ANNAPOLIS. 1772–79, 1787

Massachusetts Statehouse

In the late 1880s a movement arose in Boston to replace the cherished "Boston" statehouse, which had been designed by Charles Bulfinch in 1795 and completed three years later. Opposition from outside the city overwhelmed the effort. The capitol was restored, probably very liberally, and between 1887 and 1895 a large wing was added to the rear of what came to be called the "Bulfinch front." Designed by architects Charles Brigham and John C. Spofford, the general motif was adapted from the "colonial." Significantly, the rotunda, added in 1895, was in a style more academic than that of the rest of the wing. The Hall of Flags, as the rotunda is called, was built to honor and display Civil War battle flags and other military relics. Housed completely within the later addition and without external expression, the space provides a rotunda effect to a capitol that never had one. A great dome was part of Bulfinch's original scheme, of course; but the architect placed the General Court (house of representatives) in the central space beneath it, and there this lower house remains. His idea was copied in many New England capitols of his time and the following twenty years. But the shallow dome seen here has broader relations in many other Beaux Arts–style capitols across the country: formed in plaster and lath, encircled by electric bulbs, and decorated with stained glass. Likewise, the room it lights is finished handsomely in marble and bronze.

BOSTON. 1795–98, 1887–95

Michigan State Capitol

Elijah E. Myers saw the magnificent plans for the Illinois and Iowa statehouses and, deciding to try his hand at capitol design, entered the Michigan design competition and won. The capitol was built between 1871 and 1879, within its budget, and established Myers as an expert in public architecture. He designed the capitols of Texas and Colorado and was involved in nearly every competition from the 1870s to about 1900. Myers had a flair for the spectacular—nowhere more evident than in his rotundas. This, his first, is ringed with iron balconies carried on ornate brackets; the walls are elaborately decorated with painted effects and allegories of uncertain authorship in oil painted on canvas and fixed to the curving walls; the floor is thick glass. His capitol was lighted by fanciful gas chandeliers adorned with the state symbol, the elk; his legislative halls are like opera houses. If he did not open the Gilded Age in capitols, Myers certainly drove it full steam in designing his capitols, courthouses, and many other sorts of public buildings. The Michigan capitol remained virtually unchanged until the 1970s, when it was defaced by the horizontal subdivision of parts of the interior. Between 1986 and 1992 it underwent a complete renewal under the direction of architect Richard C. Frank and stands as the most comprehensively restored Victorian state capitol in the nation.

LANSING. 1871–79

Minnesota State Capitol

Minnesota's capitol is the best of the Beaux Arts–period statehouses. Designed by Cass Gilbert and built between 1896 and 1905, it began rather simpler than it turned out. Gilbert, a master at managing and getting along with building commissioners, won the design competition as an obscure architect; by the time the building was completed he was one of the most prominent architects in the United States. In the process of his rise, he learned a lot about the so-called American Renaissance, of which neoclassical architecture was only a part. Relocated from St. Paul to New York, he met the great muralists and sculptors, and as he got to know and admire their work, he brought them to the attention of the building commission in St. Paul. The resulting capitol is not only extremely fine in its Renaissance interpretation but also a gallery of good paintings and sculpture. A tour of this building can consume most of a day. At the base of the dome is sculptor Daniel Chester French's beautiful horses and chariot in gold-covered bronze; in the Governor's Reception Room are Frank Millet's paintings representing Minnesota's service in the Civil War, masterpieces in themselves. The dome's inner shell and its decorations show Gilbert's gifts as a designer. He worked masterfully in any historical style. Here Gilbert selected St. Peter's in Rome as the inspiration for his dome—and seems to have had no pressure to use St. Paul's instead.

ST. PAUL. 1896–1905

63

Mississippi State Capitol

By 1901 Mississippi's distinguished capitol of the 1830s was too small, so the state ordered it preserved and called for a new building for the legislature. Theodore C. Link of St. Louis designed it in the Beaux Arts style. The storms of late nineteenth-century history had swept Link, a native of Heidelberg, through architects' offices in London and Paris, where he attended the Ecole des Arts et Métièrs before migrating from a starving France to America. His gifts are seen in the heavy-arched Union Station in St. Louis. For Mississippi he designed a building monumental and traditional but also, for 1901, modern. The interior has numerous skylights, and natural light falls through glass floor tiles. The capitol is a building rich in natural light, an effect imitated in artificial lighting by thousands of exposed light bulbs in the rotunda. Black has a great presence in this building, whereas white is more usual in capitols of its time. Extensive use is made of black scagliola, set off by smaller elements in rose, ocher, and gray. The legislative halls have shallow domes with stained glass. Tall and highly decorated, the central dome crowns the rotunda, itself designed with soaring arches and galleries. Through nearly a century of use, this building has undergone little serious alteration. It was restored in the early 1980s, with some modernizations.

JACKSON. 1901–3

Missouri State Capitol

This memorable rotunda is different from all the others, having the effect of penetrating upward through a series of low vaults. Missouri's earlier capitol burned, so architects were called to Jefferson City to compete for a new building in 1913. Tracy and Swartwout of New York, a firm highly respected for its design skills, won and designed the capitol, which was completed five years later. The capitol form is masterfully rendered in precise Beaux Arts neoclassicism: its dome patterned after St. Peter's, its columned wings harkening to federal architecture of the 1920s. Interested citizens urged the building commission to establish an art program; by 1928, a decade later, more than a million dollars had been spent on murals and statuary. The rotunda was decorated by the English muralist Frank Brangwyn. His designs seem to flow from the veining of the marble walls and floors in an exquisite effect, soft in color, delicate in a weblike tracery that is carried all the way to the dome.

JEFFERSON CITY. 1913–18

Montana State Capitol

Located on a hill overlooking Helena, Montana's statehouse was built in the four years following 1898 by the local architecture firm Bell and Kent. Between 1909 and 1912 it was enlarged by Frank Mills Andrews, architect of the Kentucky capitol. Westerners liked flamboyantly colored rotundas, and nearly all their capitols had them—this, rising a hundred feet, being no exception. To the Renaissance architecture of the inner dome, executed in plaster over lath, painter C. A. Pedretti of Cincinnati added elaborate decorations, scenes of the West, and allegories, such as these four representations of Montana pioneers: the Indian chief, the miner, the trapper, and the cowboy. Elsewhere there is gilding with bronzing powder, marbleizing, wood graining, and other effects of grandeur possible with paint. Built in a city of good buildings, the Montana capitol was nevertheless a surprise to visitors when it was new. The West was won but not tamed. Through pesky local pressure, the building commissioners reluctantly hired a local artist to execute a work that they were loath to put alongside that of Professor Pedretti—but some lived to see the name of Charlie Russell outrank even that of the professor.

HELENA. 1898–1902, 1909–12

68

Nebraska State Capitol

The American architectural world was electrified in 1919 with the winning project for the Nebraska capitol competition: a tower—a skyscraper. It did not look like a capitol at all. However, Bertram Goodhue's Nebraska capitol, completed in 1932, long after his death, was more traditional than it seemed. Designed probably after the Kallio Church (1909–12) built by Lars Eliel Sonck in Helsinki a decade before, it seemed wholly modern, but the traditional capitol elements were all there, including the interior dome, which, in relation to the overall height of the tower, is a low, inner dome. Goodhue's tower as originally conceived was ornamental, like a dome; only later was it subdivided into offices. The capitol was built with an art program that was the most extensive ever known in an American statehouse, with painting, sculpture, and iron and tile work. Its power is conveyed in this central square area, where barrel vaults spring from heavy piers and pendentives rise from the corners to the dome. Although seemingly a union of stones that bear a heavy load, the structure is actually steel beams and hollow tiles with surface veneers of stone. The effect is the principal ornament of the building.

OMAHA. 1919–32

New Jersey Statehouse

If America ever had the equivalent of a European palace added onto over generations, it is the New Jersey Statehouse. Begun in 1794, it was a rectangular stone structure that looked like a courthouse. Over the next century and more it was expanded time and again into the giant, rambling building it is today, restored by architects Ford, Farewell, Mills and Gatsch. One can still climb to the attic and walk along the top of the stone walls of the original eighteenth-century structure. The rotunda, with its dome, is a section added to the rear of the 1794 statehouse by architect John Notman in 1845 and later remodeled by Samuel Sloan. It shows the architectural embellishments of Sloan: cast-iron ribs and railings and circles of restrained decorative plaster. On above, seemingly almost part of something else, the interior of the dome glows with natural light. Although central to the building, the rotunda is not foremost in one's impressions of the statehouse but rather is one in a number of rooms linked together with no apparent master plan—creating this unusual public building that has literally risen and grown with the history of the state it serves.

TRENTON. 1794, 1845, 1871–72

New Mexico State Capitol

The adobe Palace of the Governors was the first capitol of New Mexico, built in 1710 and still standing on the plaza in Santa Fe. A half dozen blocks away is the state's new capitol, completed in 1966. It seemed a stark and hard building at first, on a barren plot of land outside Santa Fe's historic district. With plantings of native trees and shrubs, this doughnut-shaped building has mellowed, and the combination of materials used inside—aluminum, brass, walnut paneling, terrazzo—somehow enjoys a pleasant cohesiveness it did not seem to have three decades ago. The architect, W. C. Kruger, was undoubtedly inspired by Frank Lloyd Wright's proposed capitol for Arizona about ten years earlier, with its ethnic symbolism, when he selected the sun symbol of the local Zia Pueblo as inspiration for the building's footprint; Wright had used a thunderbird. Before the New Mexico capitol could be built, however, various elements within artistic Santa Fe had their say. The effort to be traditional mingled adobe and Territorial styles with the building's odd round "Indian" contour, all on an improbably large scale. In keeping with the spare, streamlined detailing of the structure, the dome is all but invisible from the exterior and inside forms the shallow skylighted ceiling of the rotunda. The glow of light in the rotunda suggests in a soft tone the bright western skies outside and itself becomes an element in the architecture—in true dome tradition.

SANTA FE. 1965–66

North Carolina State Capitol

North Carolina officials in 1833 looked to New York for architects to replace their beloved statehouse of 1792–1820 that had burned. Town and Davis, the firm of the famous bridge builder and architect Ithiel Town and architect A. J. Davis, produced plans for a new capitol. It is a noble structure of stone, finely dressed, and is one of some five or six American buildings that show the Greek Revival at its most creative. The capitol commissioners, like everyone else, had admired the rotunda in the previous statehouse, so they ordered that a rotunda and dome be included. In the old building had been Antonio Canova's statue of a seated George Washington in Roman armor—alas, destroyed in the fire. Davis's design—for there is no reason to think that Town designed any of it—suggests the earlier statehouse only in its cruciform plan. The rotunda rises where the two wings cross; a circular opening in the floor, railed, admits daylight into the ground floor from the oculus above. Strangely, after 150 years, the old capitol that stood here before is still remembered somehow as having been better. Some twenty years ago the state of North Carolina located the cast for the Washington statue at Canova's studio in Possagno, Italy. It has been reproduced in marble and can be seen in the photograph. The legislature moved to a separate building in 1963, leaving the capitol, on which restoration began in 1971, for the governor's office and ceremonial and museum uses.

RALEIGH. 1833–40

Ohio Statehouse

In the dark days of the Panic of 1837, the legislators of Ohio determined to build a permanent statehouse in Columbus, not only for fireproof convenience for themselves but also to secure the capital designation for the city and end bickering over it. They selected a square in the heart of town, alongside the National Road. Architects swarmed like bees to the competition, but the winner was not an architect but the painter Thomas Cole, dean of the Hudson River School of landscape painting. Cole did not actually build the statehouse and probably did not have a clue how it might be done. A succession of architects made changes as its walls rose, yet none so radical that the design cannot be called Cole's. It is a powerful structure of stone lined with brick, load bearing, with an extensive system of brick groin vaults stacked three stories to a light trellis of iron covered with copper. The plaster-decorated dome is internal, fit into a lofty peppermill of a lantern set in the center of the roof. Apparently the plaster decoration inside the dome's shell is original, while the oculus is probably the third or fourth put there. A restoration by Schooley-Caldwell and Associates will once again fill the rotunda with natural light and patterns of color from the glass in the dome.

COLUMBUS. 1838–60

79

Oklahoma State Capitol

The Oklahoma capitol, a long Beaux Arts structure of Oklahoma pink granite and Indiana limestone, was racing for completion when World War 1 began. Patriotically, work was halted, with the idea of taking it up again when the enemy was whipped. But in the short time of the war so much changed in the world—as well as in Oklahoma City—that the building commission hesitated to build the dome. Capitols had turned to towers by 1919. A roof was put over the rotunda, and a stained-glass and plaster dome beneath it gave the appearance inside that there was a dome. Oil came in on the grounds; pumpers nodded night and day all around the crisp stone walls. For a long time a drawing of the final project hung on a wall in the capitol. It showed a dome based on Les Invalides, but it was never built. Architects Layton and Smith passed into history, and today the Oklahoma capitol remains unfinished by choice—a tombstone of the era of Beaux Arts capitols and also, in a sense, of domes.

OKLAHOMA CITY. 1914–17

Oregon State Capitol

Oregon's present capitol might never have been built had the old Victorian capitol not burned, for it was a popular building. After the fire, in the spring of 1935, the legislature authorized a new capitol. Forty-five percent of the cost was covered by the Public Works Administration, and a competition produced 123 entries. Francis Keally of New York won. His design was in the Moderne mode—classicism peeled down to the simplest lines and shapes. The central area, not so much a rotunda as a round-cornered square, is surmounted by a cupola, decorated within and admitting natural light into a streamlined interior walled in white marble and plaster. Looking at the building from the outside, with its ribbed lantern and its whiteness from so much marble, visitors have compared the Oregon capitol to a coil refrigerator of its time. But the complaint is not serious. This capitol, for all its several reflections of the Ohio statehouse, is otherwise unique—seated jewel-like on emerald green lawns, with sympathetically designed office buildings along its mall, often curtained in northwestern rain.

SALEM. 1936–38

Pennsylvania State Capitol

This dome is only one of the many splendors of the statehouse in Harrisburg. The capitol was conceived by the building commission in 1898 to be the most magnificent state capitol in the United States. The architect, Joseph M. Huston, took his dome from St. Peter's and gave it great mass as well as a dressing of mural art, marble, glass tiles, and gilded torchères gleaming with electric bulbs. The great weight of the dome—estimated at fifty-two million pounds—is carried on four pillars, footed seven feet into a natural slate bed, that taper from twenty-nine feet at the base to twelve feet at the top. Grand stairs in white marble rise in the rotunda; they are patterned on those in the Paris Opera House. No art program had ever been this extensive. Leading muralists of the day, such as Edwin Austin Abbey and Violett Oakley, were called to the work. Their art is a wonder to see now, nearly a hundred years later; the lunettes are by Abbey, a Pennsylvanian, as are the gold medallions, which represent religion, science, law, and art. Outside, sculpture groups by George Gray Barnard adorned the entrances. When the capitol was completed in 1907 special trains took thousands of weekend visitors from Philadelphia to see the legislative marvel. It remains today virtually as it has always been—a little worn by time but surely America's most memorable monument to democracy's sometimes flamboyant tendency to glory in architecture.

HARRISBURG. 1898–1907

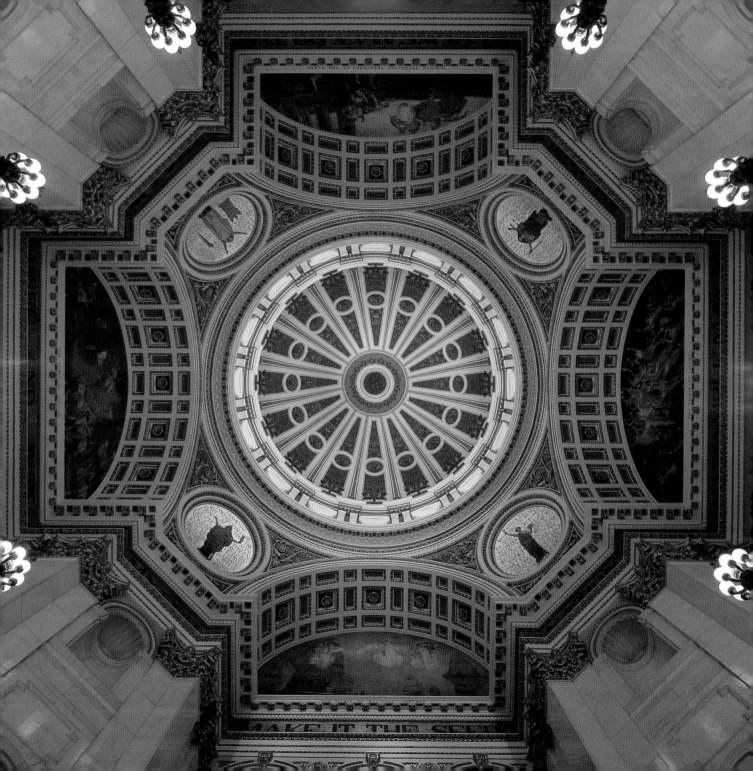

Rhode Island State Capitol

Before this capitol was completed in 1905, Rhode Island had two capitals, used alternately: Newport and Providence. With the building of the capitol, Providence won out and became the permanent seat of government. The elegant, snowy marble statehouse is the only one designed in its entirety by McKim, Mead and White, the leading Beaux Arts architecture practice in the nation. Charles McKim was the principal on this project and claimed that he took some of his ideas from John McComb and Joseph F. Mangin's old New York City Hall (1802). The rotunda houses marble stairs by which one ascends higher into the white marble interior through gradual ranges of steps and broad landings. It is not the welcoming rotunda of the midwestern capitols but a ceremonial place where, in being forced to climb, one joins in the ceremony. Color is used inside with great restraint. Openings that allow the flow of natural light are masterfully designed, giving the rotunda a constant play of light, even on dark days.

PROVIDENCE. 1895–1905

South Carolina Statehouse

South Carolina's capitol, where Union cannon balls are still lodged in the walls, symbolizes the state's history in grand ambitions snuffed out by the Civil War and its dismal aftermath, which in a sense dragged on for a century. First there was a wooden statehouse on this site, toward the close of the 1780s. In 1853 it was simply rolled aside to make way for a new marble capitol, which was to have not a dome but a tall, monumental tower patterned probably on the Leeds Town Hall in England, designed by Cuthbert Brodrick also in the 1850s. The architect, John R. Niernsee of Baltimore, won a controversial national design competition, and work began in 1854. The shell was complete in 1865, when General Sherman led his army up from Georgia. Parts of Columbia were burned, including the old statehouse. After the Civil War an impoverished state legislature gradually swept up funds to complete the building with a temporary roof and moved inside. Hard times continued; nevertheless, between 1902 and 1907 the well-known railroad architect Frank P. Milburn "finished" the statehouse with a copper dome and extensive pressed metal architectural elements within. From the outside the dome, mounted on the rich, heavy stone walls, seems small and inconsequential. Inside, in the vast central space that would have been graced by vaults and colonnades and lighted by the tower, the opening of the dome is little more impressive than a skylight, the natural light supplemented by modern down lights, its decorations hardly noticed in the grand volume of the room below.

COLUMBIA. 1854–65, 1902–7

South Dakota State Capitol

Set in the little city of Pierre, the South Dakota capitol was completed in 1910, with a wing added two decades later. It was patterned on the popular capitol of Montana, but many of the apparent faults of that building were discarded and the general concept improved on by architect M. E. Bell. The entire exterior seems to exist for the dome: the central block steps up to it, terminating at its colonnaded drum with richly carved pediments. The dome, sheathed in copper, combines many neoclassical elements together with columns and corner niches of stone. Decoration on the interior is more restrained than in Montana yet not much simpler. Edward Simmons's painted roundels are allegories of mining, agriculture, ranching, and the family, all set against brilliant gold. Seals represent Spain, France, the United States, and South Dakota, whose flags have flown over the state. An amber glow pervades the interior when sunlight falls through the stained-glass windows.

PIERRE. 1907–10, 1934

Tennessee State Capitol

Tennessee was late in building a statehouse: it had been a state for nearly a half century when the decision was made in 1844. Work commenced in 1845 and continued until the close of 1859. Many architects were interviewed, but when it became evident that the celebrated William Strickland, dean of architects at the time, might be available, the building commissioners could see none but him. The old man moved from Philadelphia, where he was no longer fashionable, to Nashville, where he was welcomed as a great artist. Tennessee's soaring, towered capitol was to be his valedictory as well as his tomb, for his coffin is sealed in one of the porticoes. As architecture the building has some truly sublime moments. In this central crossing—not a rotunda—four colossal arches of Tennessee marble climax in a groin vault. The view here hints at the structural magnificence that characterizes the rest of the capitol. Spanning the large crossing below, the dressed limestone and the vault are the overpowering ornaments of this soaring union of structural forces. A reproduction of the original 1850s gas chandelier hangs from the center. Decorative painting installed during the late 1950s to imitate work from 1857 was supervised by muralist Allyn Cox. Refurbishment of some of the interiors along historical lines has been carried out by architects Mesick, Cohen and Waite. Strickland's appetite for vaulting was almost Roman in its extent. Here he designed in a mode that had made him famous but was long out of style—the victim of advanced technology and the accompanying taste for applied decoration.

NASHVILLE. 1845–59

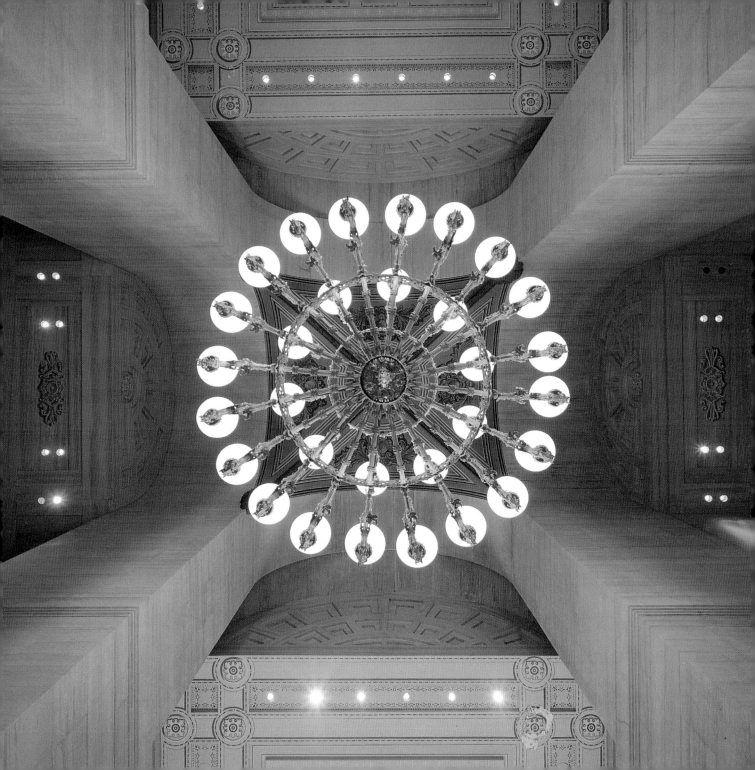

Texas State Capitol

Naturally the Texas capitol would be expected to be taller than all the others; although not yet proven by steel tape and one-by-one comparison, the boast is often made. This building is one of Elijah E. Myers's opulent creations, built for Texas by Chicago businessmen in exchange for several million acres of west Texas ranch lands. The capitol is constructed of the beautiful, rose-red granite from north of Marble Falls, Texas; pressed tin and cast iron, painted to match the granite, form the walls in high places. While there is, of course, an inner dome, one wonders how any inner dome could be conceived to rise so high. The eye struggles to reach the top, where a gilded Lone Star shines 260 feet above the floor. Visiting schoolchildren share legends of janitors' falling to grizzly deaths while changing the single light bulb that dangles from the star. Ringed by balconies that open off the various levels of the building, the rotunda is the most spellbinding in the United States; unabashed in scale, it shows no restraint to the viewer, no mercy to the vertiginous. The student of state capitols cannot help but draw an analogy between this thunderously grand statehouse and Maryland's of a century before. Builders of both reached about as high with their domes as the technology of their times allowed; yet the one in Annapolis was probably the most wondrous when it was new, for already by the 1880s commercial buildings rivaled the height of the capitol domes that had once dominated the landscape. As the earlier capitol was the self-appointed symbol of a new nation, the Texas capitol is an enduring symbol of the development of the West—a dividing point between the wooded America that stretched back to Maine and the great, open plains.

AUSTIN. 1882–88

Utah State Capitol

Brigham Young, who was also a cabinetmaker, and architect Truman O. Angell set architectural standards high in Salt Lake City in the 1840s. When Richard Kletting designed the new capitol in 1913, he had to compete in a city with numerous fine specimens of architecture, not the least Angell and Young's Mormon Temple (1853). Kletting was German by birth, educated in architecture in Munich, Vienna, and Paris. His vision was European, and he saw this capitol as part of a City Beautiful scheme. It is a building instead left much to itself in an elevated setting, a colonnaded temple-style structure surmounted by a monumental dome. The monolithic columns of marble become almost opal-like—translucent—in the light at the beginning and ending of each day. Beneath the monumental dome the spectacular rotunda grants all the magnificence the exterior has promised, seen from long distances, across the landscape. The artists who created its historical art are described as out-of-work Depression-era painters. The Dominguez-Escalante Expedition from Mexico is depicted at lower right; John Frémont, upper right, is shown at his first sight of the Great Salt Lake; Peter Skene Ogden is seen on the Snake River, upper left; and, at lower left, Brigham Young and his Mormon "saints" in 1847 enter the valley they will in a short time transform into a garden.

SALT LAKE CITY. 1913–16

Virginia State Capitol

While the guns of the Revolution were still smoking, Gov. Thomas Jefferson designed a capitol for Virginia in imitation of the Maison Carrée, a Roman temple in Nîmes, France. A decade later, serving as American minister to France, he visited the temple for the first time and modified his plans, sending them, with a plaster model, back to Richmond. He changed the column order from Corinthian to Ionic, as a realistic measure to accommodate the limits of American stonecraft, and plaster on brick replaced dressed stone. When the legislature got the plans, it had already laid the foundation for a capitol patterned on the one it had abandoned in Williamsburg. But through James Madison's influence Jefferson's plan was adapted to what already stood. The temple capitol rose between 1787 and 1799, and the result, if somewhat curious, was generally well received even by Jefferson himself. The dome is entirely an interior feature curving up into the attic. Beneath it the legislature in the 1790s placed Jean Antoine Houdon's full-length statue of George Washington, carved in marble to actual size from measurements made of the man. Most of the interior of the capitol was destroyed in 1909, when structural weakness and a need for more space moved the commonwealth to rebuild it within its shell and add wings. The dome attempts to duplicate the original, a confection in plaster with nineteenth-century–style decoration.

RICHMOND. 1787–99, 1909

Washington State Capitol

Projects for new state capitols found ready enthusiasm from designers who worked in the Beaux Arts style—all the more among those favoring improved city plans to honor their buildings, with parks and great public buildings. At the suggestion of New York architect Ernest Flagg, the state of Washington decided to build a government campus rather than just a capitol, something "reminiscent of the Acropolis at Athens." Jefferson had envisioned this for the hills of Richmond. But no capitol site is as wonderful in scenic beauty as the one set aside in Olympia. Flagg was replaced in 1909 by Walter R. Wilder and Harry K. White, who developed a master plan including the capitol or legislative building, begun in 1912. Four buildings of this western Acropolis were completed by the mid-1920s. The Legislative Hall, the sixth, is a heavy building dominated by its dome. Elevated above the rest of the complex, its dome is patterned after the one on St. Peter's. A walk through the unseen space between the inner shell and the outer dome reveals vastness and vacantness, with perilous wooden catwalks passing through it. The inner shell is ornamented in plaster with gilt, but with restraint; the dome is painted cobalt blue at the apex. One wonders what Olympia's great government complex might have been had it been realized. Like many Beaux Arts ideas, the City Beautiful concept popularized by the 1893 World's Columbian Exposition in Chicago died with World War I. Olympia's proposed Acropolis died, too, and remains only partially built, devoid of the avenues and parks that would have surrounded it and now encumbered by obtrusive construction.

OLYMPIA. 1912–28

West Virginia State Capitol

Traveling through the mountains of West Virginia there is no greater surprise than on reaching Charleston, when the state capitol suddenly appears. It stands in the bosom of the riverside city, surrounded by mature trees. The last of the great Beaux Arts capitols, it was built long after its time, rising part by part and finished in 1932. Cass Gilbert was the architect in name, but his son Cass Gilbert, Jr., was in fact the architect, and the building shows that the father's sensitivity to detail was passed on to the son. The stonework is fine and delicate, suggesting French masonry and carving of the eighteenth century, and contributes to the French feeling of the architecture of this state-house. Patterned on St. Paul's, the dome is constructed of steel finished in stone with a gilded metal roof. The rotunda beneath it is large and heavy, adorned with a four-thousand-pound, hundred-light spherical chandelier, which is lowered just before every inauguration, its ten thousand glass pieces cleaned and polished. Finished entirely in highly figured white marble, the rotunda rises in a Piranesian sort of masonry splendor that, even in the 1930s, seemed ambitious in the context of the mountain town and its rambling river.

CHARLESTON. 1930–32

Wisconsin State Capitol

By tradition dating to the 1850s, Wisconsin's capitols have been in the shape of a Greek cross. The first version stood from 1856 until 1913, when it was replaced by the present monumental structure by George B. Post of New York. Executed in the richest materials, the statehouse has little ground between it and the busy capital and university town of Madison that surrounds it. Pioneers built the original capitol among the businesses and commercial interests for convenience. A new location outside town was considered, but it was dropped in favor of leaving the capitol in the heart of things. When finished it loomed and leered over the townscape, its bronze and marble figures looking down on two-story buildings and narrow streets. The architect carefully designed this capitol to be a monument from a distance, approaching town, yet to address town life in the scale of the lower part. It owes much of its capitol personality to the crowded site. The rotunda is the thoroughfare of Madison, resplendent in historical murals by Edwin H. Blashfield, Hugo Ballin, and Albert Herter, who for accuracy painted them under the supervision of the history department at the University of Wisconsin. Kenyon Cox's allegorical murals adorn the dome's pendentives like jewelry, set among many kinds of marble and abundant gold leaf, while Blashfield's Resources of Wisconsin above spans the thirty-four-foot ceiling of the dome, two hundred feet above the rotunda's colored granite floor.

MADISON. 1906–17

Wyoming State Capitol

Plans for this capitol were called for in 1886 from two architects: Elijah E. Myers—for the building commissioners admired his new Texas capitol—and David W. Gibbs of Toledo, Ohio. Gibbs won with a much-reduced version, externally, of Myers's capitol in Austin, to Myers's great chagrin. Cheyenne was a well-planned little city, and the capitol became its crown. Most people arrived by train. Visitors walked through the Union Pacific depot and at its great arched entrance looked down Capitol Avenue to the statehouse at the other end. The view was impressive, with trees planted along the sides and neat houses and stores backed by a windswept landscape. It is a delightful capitol built of reddish stone, its dome patterned somewhat on Les Invalides. A great flourish of steps carries the visitor beneath a high-flown porch into the capitol's interior, where the rotunda, although not quite domestic scale, is perhaps hotel scale and embellished with marbleized plaster columns, cherry wood balustrades, and some ornamental stenciling and neo-classical ornament in plaster. Offices of four of Wyoming's five elected state officials open off this rotunda.

CHEYENNE. 1886–90, 1915